1,000,000 Books

are available to read at

Forgotten Books

www.ForgottenBooks.com

Read online
Download PDF
Purchase in print

ISBN 978-0-332-06051-4
PIBN 11212670

This book is a reproduction of an important historical work. Forgotten Books uses state-of-the-art technology to digitally reconstruct the work, preserving the original format whilst repairing imperfections present in the aged copy. In rare cases, an imperfection in the original, such as a blemish or missing page, may be replicated in our edition. We do, however, repair the vast majority of imperfections successfully; any imperfections that remain are intentionally left to preserve the state of such historical works.

Forgotten Books is a registered trademark of FB &c Ltd.
Copyright © 2018 FB &c Ltd.
FB &c Ltd, Dalton House, 60 Windsor Avenue, London, SW19 2RR.
Company number 08720141. Registered in England and Wales.

For support please visit www.forgottenbooks.com

1 MONTH OF FREE READING

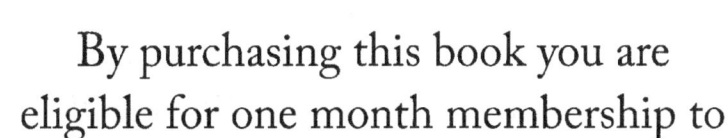

at

www.ForgottenBooks.com

By purchasing this book you are eligible for one month membership to ForgottenBooks.com, giving you unlimited access to our entire collection of over 1,000,000 titles via our web site and mobile apps.

To claim your free month visit: www.forgottenbooks.com/free1212670

*Offer is valid for 45 days from date of purchase. Terms and conditions apply.

English
Français
Deutsche
Italiano
Español
Português

www.forgottenbooks.com

Mythology Photography **Fiction** Fishing Christianity **Art** Cooking Essays Buddhism Freemasonry Medicine **Biology** Music **Ancient Egypt** Evolution Carpentry Physics Dance Geology **Mathematics** Fitness Shakespeare **Folklore** Yoga Marketing **Confidence** Immortality Biographies Poetry **Psychology** Witchcraft Electronics Chemistry History **Law** Accounting **Philosophy** Anthropology Alchemy Drama Quantum Mechanics Atheism Sexual Health **Ancient History Entrepreneurship** Languages Sport Paleontology Needlework Islam **Metaphysics** Investment Archaeology Parenting Statistics Criminology
Motivational

DR. TICKNOR'S ADDRESS

TO THE

CANDIDATES

FOR

DEGREES AND LICENSES,

IN THE

MEDICAL INSTITUTION OF YALE COLLEGE,

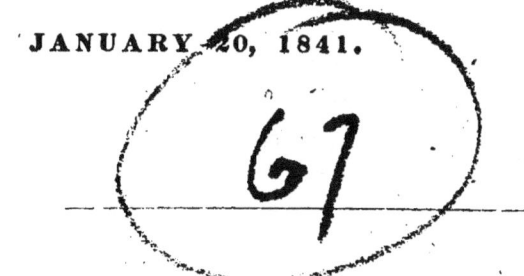

JANUARY 20, 1841.

THE ANNUAL ADDRESS

TO THE

CANDIDATES

FOR

DEGREES AND LICENSES,

IN THE

MEDICAL INSTITUTION OF YALE COLLEGE,

JANUARY 20, 1841.

BY LUTHER TICKNOR, M. D.

MEMBER OF THE BOARD OF EXAMINATION.

PUBLISHED AT THE REQUEST OF THE CLASS.

NEW HAVEN:
PRINTED BY B. L. HAMLEN.

1841.

ADDRESS.

Gentlemen,

Having gone through with private and public instruction, and in so doing complied with the prescribed formalities of a medical education, and being about to assume the guardianship of public health, it is no more than fair to presume you are worthy to be received into the medical family. If you have been zealous, devoted students; if your studies have occupied your time, engrossed your attention, and called into exercise all the energies of your minds, as they certainly should; still are you probably ignorant, at least to some extent, of the character and habits of that society to which you are about to be introduced, so far as its prominent traits are interesting to men of our profession. A few brief hints, then, on this subject may not be amiss, since a misapprehension, or error in the outset, frequently mars a man's whole history, and involves consequences which are not easily counteracted, nor always patiently endured.

Having no test by which to estimate his claims to patronage, the public, though courteous and civil enough, are apt to be guarded and cautious, shy, and sometimes fickle minded; and only receive into full favor and confidence, a young physician, when he shall have given some fair evidence of cleverness in his profession. The public you are about to serve, are ignorant of medicine as a science; they know little or nothing of its first principles; caring little about the formalities of medical education, and still less for college honors. Though men do not now believe in witchcraft, and dare to be skeptical in regard to some of the grosser superstitions connected with the art of healing; yet there is scarcely a theory so absurd, or a proposition so ill supported, that they will not embrace it; or a nostrum so knavishly got up, that they will not swallow it, if offered and recommended by an uneducated pretender to medical skill. This infatuation, this exaltation of the believing faculty, is not confined to men of narrow, uncultivated minds; nor is it the "besetting sin" of any particular class of your fellow-citizens—it is not confined to caste, nor district, nor country. A belief that a panacea, a universal remedy for all human ills, is already discovered, or an expectation that such a disclosure is about to be made, seems to be prevalent among us, affecting those who minister at the altar, and members of the bar; those entrusted with legislation, and the honorable offices of the bench, as well as the humble and less privileged members of the community; and, to our great mortification, they expect this discovery to be made by any other man, than a regularly educated physician. Talented and gifted men, and men in "high places," are not always wise men; their discernment of merit, or their opinions on subjects connected with medicine, are sometimes no more worthy of respect than those of the humblest minds in the community. You are as likely to find the former swallowing lobelia and matchless sanative, as the latter.

Another characteristic of society, to which I will call your attention, that you may be prepared to meet it with an undisturbed spirit, is ingratitude. Men in all latitudes, and under all degrees of cultivation, are rendered unhappy by a sense of obligation created by benefits, and will seek relief by depreciating the benefit. I do not mean that this is true of all men, without exception, for there are many honorable instances to the contrary; but man is an ungrateful creature, and will not long abide a feeling of indebtedness. But, be this as it may, this world has not yet established a character for adequately rewarding her benefactors; and you will be disappointed, if you expect even your most successful and expensive services to meet the reward of a grateful heart; and you will have cause for thankfulness, if your reasonable bills are paid without murmuring. A great proportion of those who have devoted all their powers and sacrificed their lives to the service of their fellow men, have gone down to the grave unthanked and unblessed, and not unfrequently reproached. Be ye, then, neither disappointed nor discouraged, when your professional labors are repaid with neglect, your motives impugned, your character traduced, and even pecuniary compensation refused, or yielded with reluctance; for so have multitudes, who have gone before you, been treated, by those from whom better things might have been expected.

Another evil exists in society, to a greater extent, perhaps, than you are aware of; an increasing consumption of stimulating and narcotic drugs, even where the various forms of alcohol have been laid aside. This is a practice fraught with danger to health and morals; and is only to be successfully met in its incipient stage. Against this foe to humanity, it is hoped you will lend your influence, both by precept and example; always prescribing cautiously, lest you inadvertently add to the number of cachectic cases, and swell the catalogue of "opium eaters."

Let me now, gentlemen, call your attention to a few brief remarks concerning the character you are to form, the duties that are expected from you, and the burdens you are to bear, if you go forward in this enterprise; for you commence practice without professional character, and doubtless are desirous of early acquiring a professional reputation, which shall distinguish you from others, and place you above your fellows. The study of medicine, in most, if not all its departments, while it has been laborious and imposed much self-denial, has also mingled pleasure with labor, in disclosing the works of nature and the ways of nature's God. Another source of enjoyment, or circumstance attending your pursuits as students, is the society of each other, with all the agreeable associations of companionship, whose kind, cheering, and sustaining influence is now about to be suspended; and since the places you are about to occupy involve new duties, new responsibilities and relations, with which you are not familiar, you will stand in need of some new or additional stimulus to urge you forward in duty, and secure to your patients all your resources. Such is found in benevolence, the principle of "good will to men," in habitual, vigorous exercise; and without its influence, I fancy you will find the practice of physic very unsatisfactory. If this attribute of character is rather stinted, as an endowment, it must be cultivated, for it is a quality almost indispensable to the comfortable and successful exercise of your profession.

The acquisition of wealth, the prospect of accumulated gains, impels most men to action; for this they compass sea and land, forego domestic quiet and all the enjoyments of home; for this they trespass on the dearest rights of each other, and outrage the laws of God and man; to secure the "mammon of unrighteousness," they shut the door upon the needy, oppress the widow, and make the fatherless feel they have no friend this side of Heaven. They stifle the upbraidings of conscience, suppress the risings of humanity, and put the salvation of their souls to sale for lucre. Do not expect to make your fortunes, my young brethren, by the practice of medicine; for very few have become rich by that alone, and those not always the most worthy and useful men. I might furnish a list of names of illustrious "men of medicine," who lived and labored under pecuniary embarrassments, and died insolvent. Again, I urge you to submit to the dictates of benevolence, and subordinate every desire and interest to the simple business of doing good to your fellow-men, by the fact that many of those who will require your services, have, by their vices, placed themselves almost beyond human sympathy, outsinned human forbearance, and become nuisances and burdens upon society. What justifiable motive, think you, but benevolence, will secure to such objects a prolonged, expensive and painful attendance? They need it—they must have it—and there is a sense in which they deserve it. See to it, then, that they have your best attention, and that you do not even prescribe until you can regard those wretched, helpless objects, with fraternal feelings, and make them seem as near relatives, for they indeed are so. Unless you do this, you are unfit to act as physicians to a numerous class of your fellow-beings. I need not tell you of the claims of the virtuous poor, the unfortunate, the widow and fatherless; for if a grateful return is experienced from any, to cheer and gladden your hearts, I apprehend it will be from this class of patients. To such, their physician seems like a friend, a benefactor, a brother.

I think there can be no question, that a benevolent, enterprising physician, will find business and bread; but beyond a bare support, he has little to expect.

Another quality of character which you will find very important in professional business, is firmness, or the power of subjecting your conduct to the government of your own judgment. Some men are very gifted in this particular, making uncomfortable neighbors, and not unfrequently dangerous physicians. This pride of opinion you will of course avoid, and at the same time cultivate that reliance upon your own judgment, which shall make your practice your own; for, unless you early possess this power, you will certainly be defeated in your undertaking, disappoint your friends, and become the property of others, and the sport of your enemies. Some of you, at least, may be conscious of deficiency in this, as a natural attribute; if so, let me tell you, that with many men this power is an acquisition rather than a gift, and is susceptible of very extensive cultivation. I would therefore advise you to guard against temerity on the one hand, and timidity and weakness on the other, which have proved fatal to the fair prospects of many young men.

Another attainment, which I will mention in this place, as possessing great value to a physician, is the habit of expecting much from the resources of nature, aided by well directed efforts. This expecting, this "hoping for better times," has done much in our world; whereas despondency over a case, the opposite feeling, is dangerous to both physician and patient, frequently proving fatal to the former, if not to the latter. This assurance of success, however, ought to be borne with great modesty—strongly felt, and cautiously expressed. In urging upon you a firm, enlarged expectation of success, I by no means wish to encourage a fool-hardy, reckless, headlong confidence, in those cases whose responsibilities should always be divided, when practicable, with the senior members of the profession.

To benevolence, or love of your fellow-men, "which many waters can not quench," and which "endureth all things," sustained by firmness of purpose, and endorsed by elevated expectations from nature and art, you will add habits of industry, in following up professional studies. It is almost certainly fatal to the prospects of young men, to suppose an adequate stock of knowledge is already acquired, and that nothing remains to be done but to give it a practical shape and enjoy the income. Very few, perhaps not any, would admit this in theory, and yet how many, too many alas! carry it out in practice! If your training, if your professional studies end here, woe to your patients, woe to those communities over whose health you may be called to preside! I do not say you can not be useful, and even eminent in your calling, and neglect some of those sciences auxiliary to the healing art; but I do say, you ought to cultivate, with unwearied industry, first of all, and most of all, pathology. In this department, more than any other, lies the "great strength" of a physician. A man so familiar with morbid phenomena, as readily to detect the seat, character and stage of a disease, and able with tolerable certainty to anticipate its progress and result, possesses an enviable talent, and is a giant in his profession, whatever may have been his opportunities in early life. In addition to books, which you will find necessary to correct your errors and enlarge your views, you will have recourse to laborious investigations and painful vigilance over the development of symptoms and effects of remedies, as of the first importance. I would recommend not merely a courteous, gentlemanly attention to the sick, but such a deep, affectionate interest in every thing pertaining to a case, that nothing important shall elude observation or escape the memory. It is best, I think, to review often the history of a case; investigate again and again, even though you should appear uninspired and less profoundly learned than you could wish. Let no consideration whatever deter you from making thorough work in pathology. For this purpose, it is generally best to listen, at least, to all that may be said of a case, by those knowing, meddling, officious persons, who abound in every country village; for if you receive no useful hint, or obtain no other information, you will be apt to learn the character and consequence of those individuals, who may on some occasions give you trouble. Again, mothers are not often good prescribers, but they are acute observers, and their observations are always worthy of attention, and frequently of very great respect; for they are prompted by the strongest feelings known to our fallen nature. If, therefore, you are able, by unwearied observations of your own, and by taking those of others for what they are worth, to form correct pathological opinions, your therapeutical duties will often be very light. A club or a stone is sometimes a sufficient weapon for an enemy in full view, whose character and habits are well known, while the most skillful and scientific maneuvering, and the most formidable array of artillery, may not succeed against an invisible foe, whose character, habits and resources are ill understood. It is hoped you will not come short in this department of medicine, which is imperfectly taught in books and lectures. From the nature of it, it can not be taught, but must be learned.

Some nosological arrangement, the speaker believes, should be adopted, to assist the mind in its researches, and afford accommodation as a sort of storehouse for your observations. That of Cullen, Good, or any other system, recommended by your teachers, may be used, so far as shall harmonize with your own experience, and square with the dictates of common sense.

I propose to address to you, a few remarks, relative to the mistakes and errors of young physicians; because their consequences are frequently of a most serious and lasting character. And first, be exceedingly guarded against considering yourselves the most learned men in the profession; and, that those who have gone before you, were ignorant, unsuccessful, untrustworthy men; which may indeed be true of some, but not of all. All, or nearly all the knowledge you have acquired, has been the property of others, and has been successfully employed in behalf of suffering humanity, by men of gigantic minds. Let not the magnitude of your acquirements, therefore, though they may be highly honorable to you, nor the novelty of your position in society, cherish a very confident expectation, that remedies will always do your bidding, or that diseases will always obsequiously acknowledge your approach. Modest pretensions, and cautious, guarded promises are quite compatible with a firm, determined course of practice; and will save you many a cause for blushing, deep mortification and bitter disappointment.

It would be strange if I should fail, on this occasion, to manifest some interest in behalf of your senior brethren, who have grown gray in that field which you are about to enter with such buoyant hopes and expectations of renown. Let me assure you, they have the power to do you good, and will be apt to use it for your benefit, if treated with courtesy and respect. The rules of etiquette agreed upon in this and most other medical societies, are at once the dictates of courtesy and common sense; and have for their ultimate object, the public good, and the peace and harmony of the medical profession. Hence, upon the whole, the straight-laced police of our profession, with all its inconveniences, is worthy of your observance; notwithstanding it may occasionally step between you and a rival, or intercept some temporary advantage. Next to personal honor, have in keeping the honor of your profession; as you respect your own character, so respect the character of your medical brethren. You have common interests and common feelings; are exposed to common temptations and trials; meet with common misfortunes, and war with a common enemy. Is success joyous to you? And does the voice of praise gladden your heart? Remember thy brother is but a man, and shares in this common weakness of our nature. I therefore recommend, while I admit it a high and rare attainment, to rejoice in the prosperity of a brother, and avoid bitterness towards even a rival.

Another besetting infirmity of young men, is a desire to commence life with an extensive business, a snug income and a popular reputation. This evil gives rise to others of mischievous tendencies; an overweening sensitiveness of character; a sleepless anxiety lest this or that event should be so understood as to operate against them, or seized upon and used to their hurt, in such a way, that they can neither repel it, nor counteract its influence. This morbid sensibility is increased by indulgence, and is exceedingly distressing, as well as unprofitable to him who suffers it; and more than this, it occasions the death of many an unfortunate patient. Professional enemies you may expect without hope of disappointment; but danger to your characters will doubtless arise from your own imprudence, or that of your ardent friends, rather than from those. Guard, then, with prayerful vigilance, the temper of your hearts, and the moral quality of your conduct; and the public, under the guardianship of Divine Providence, will take care of your characters. That professional character which calls for perpetual dosing and nursing, and dreads every change of weather, and variation of temperature, to say the least, is a very sickly, unpromising concern, and not likely to pay the expense of raising. Go forward, then, in all the dignity and manly vigor of public benefactors; expecting to have your motives impugned, your conduct misrepresented, your good evil spoken of, and sometimes, too, your mistakes mercifully concealed.

Again, let me invite your attention, for a moment, to those arts and tricks—the contemptible juggling and finessing—by which some men in the profession, as well as a vast multitude out of it, seek to forestall public opinion, and bespeak patronage and support. Among their artifices, are, reporting cases more or less dangerous than they are believed to be, calling them by new or unintelligible names, pretending to have discovered a new remedy or a new symptom, taking advantage of an alarmed patient or friends, a display of learning calculated to take with a certain class of people, and secrecy concerning the composition or cost of remedies, as though others did not possess them. Now, gentlemen, while these and a thousand similar arts are resorted to by men within the pale of medicine, neither the most learned discussions, nor the loudest denunciations against unprincipled pretenders to the healing art, can be expected to succeed. How contemptible in a physician, and a graduate too, to ride at the top of his speed, to throw himself into a sick room, out of breath, and with indications of profound learning and deep penetration, announce the astounding intelligence, " that he is probably too late ; but that, if there is any hope, any chance for the poor patient, he is the only man invested with adequate powers to meet the exigency." Nothing should protect men, who resort to such means for self-advancement, or self-defense, from the charge of quackery: nay more, it is piracy! Man is a sinning, and therefore a suffering and dying creature, and theorize ever so wisely, and dream ever so long and sagely, our art will not always deprive death of his victims. It proposes to lessen human suffering, and prolong human life; not to perpetuate it.

Once more; I consider it ominous of evil to all young men, setting out in life, to form a high relish for the light, dissipating literature of the day; but in a young physician, it is doubly unfortunate, if not even criminal, to spend late hours over the silly, catch-penny trash, at present so abundant, and yet so fascinating. Such a physician's fortune, I fancy, might be told, without reference to phrenological indications. All your time, all the energies of your mind, must be put in requisition, for all the resources of which you can acquire possession, will be wanted, as you advance in your professional career. If you succeed well in the practice of medicine, I suspect you will hardly find time and opportunity for much light reading, or any other fashionable mode of dissipation; nor even to make good your claims to political orthodoxy. When once public confidence is secured, a professional character established, and more especially when years of hard service begin to tell upon the constitution, physicians are strongly tempted to feel less interested in business matters, to manifest some reluctance to encounter hardships and privations, and so fall back upon their character for faithfulness and punctuality. This, the public will not bear with a very good grace, howsoever forbearing they may be towards men of other professions and pursuits. So then, if you begin your career with prompt obedience to calls, and secure a firm standing by rendering your services with cheerfulness and apparent thankfulness; thus you must do, and thus you must appear, so long as you make practice a business, or finally lose that confidence and standing.

I hope you will avoid a common mistake, that of preferring the applause of the public to the esteem and respect of the medical family, who alone are capable of duly appreciating your merit, and doing you lasting honor. The former require a long acquaintance to form a correct opinion—the latter, rarely, if ever, form a wrong one.

In conclusion, I make no apology, gentlemen, for calling your attention to the subject of religion. We have great occasion for thankfulness, that the period has gone by, as we hope, never to return, when infidelity, skepticism, or even any species of dissipation, is considered an essential item in the character of a physician; and that such a state of society now exists, that a member of our profession is hardly less esteemed for being a man of prayer. In the present state of society, you dare do no less than pay a respectful regard to religion and religious institutions; but this is far too little, and will by no means meet the wants of society, or the claims of its Divine Author. You need not capitulate, however, by attaching yourselves to a religious sect, espousing its cause, and supporting its claims to orthodoxy, by unbecoming and unprofitable controversy. The church has already engaged her best energies, and choicest talents, in controversies of, at best, very doubtful tendencies. While multitudes are contending for the faith, it is to be feared that very few are following after that "holiness without which no man can see the Lord," and exhibiting in their lives and conversation the legitimate fruits of the Spirit. Dishonor not this Institution, whose influence on learning is so extensively felt, and whose power and healthy energies in behalf of the Christian religion are so universally acknowledged, by any irregularity of life, or moral obliquity of character. Take daily counsel of the Holy Bible, and make religion, what indeed it should be, a daily, practical, personal concern; and let its influence tell upon your hearts, and be manifested in all your business transactions, and in all your intercourse with your fellow men. I trust I do not say too much, when I tell you, that on some occasions you will find, in professional life, the Bible teaching the best system of "theory and practice," affording the most efficient remedies, and certainly proposing the only unexceptionable system of "hygiene." "Godliness has the promise of the life that now is, and of that which is to come." The man, whose hopes and treasures are in heaven, is more likely to survive a severe disease, and attain to great longevity, than he whose treasure is all in this world.

Again, it is desirable that you should be firm, practical followers of the Lord Jesus; because there is a fearfully increasing tendency on the part of Christians, to an unconditional conformity to worldly maxims and customs. Let it not be so with you; be conscientious, be firm, be consistent, be stereotyped in your religion. Moral cowardice is both apostacy and treachery at once, and confers unenviable distinction on many a man at the present day.

Leave civil honors and emoluments, and the crowns of political martyrdom, to those who covet them, and aspire to no higher dignity than that conferred by a life used up in the service of your fellow men.

Without those resources, furnished by the religion of the cross, how can you gird yourselves? from what source supply armor for the conflict you are about to wage with sin and suffering, disease and death? Without religion, whither will you go for relief and support under peculiar trials, and where leave your burdens, almost great enough to crush an angel? To what source of consolation will you direct the widow and fatherless, and your suffering and dying fellow-sinner, if strangers to the Bible, and its life-giving spirit? If you confer upon society the influence of Christian example, in addition to well-directed professional services, then may you have the satisfaction of having endeavored to be faithful over a few things; and though ye shall "in many things offend," and in all come short, it is the prayer of the speaker, that you may, through the merits of our common Lord, be received into that world, where neither sin, nor disease, nor death shall ever come.

CPSIA information can be obtained
at www.ICGtesting.com
Printed in the USA
BVHW040823220219
540922BV00024B/2943/P